WHAT PROTESTANTS NEED TO KNOW ABOUT ROMAN CATHOLICS

ROBERT R. LAROCHELLE

Energion Publications
Gonzalez, FL
2013

ISBN10: 1-938434-77-0
ISBN13: 978-1-938434-77-8

Energion Publications
P. O. Box 841
Gonzalez, FL 32560

energionpubs.com
pubs@energion.com

WHY THIS BOOK

Something has motivated you to pick up this little book and to start reading it. Perhaps you are a Protestant who is in a relationship with someone who is Roman Catholic and different questions about religion have come up between you. It might even be possible that these questions could entail a more serious exploration regarding the religious upbringing of children. Maybe you have been to a recent service at a Catholic Church—a baptism, a wedding, a funeral, or First Communion—and you have found yourself asking a lot of questions.

I imagine that some of you may have considerable doubts and questions about your own religious upbringing as a Protestant and are in the process of seeking more information about other church options. As I write this, I would also expect that some folks reading it may have found the new Pope, Francis I, to be fascinating and are taking a fresh look at Catholicism because of the positive regard they have for him. I would suspect as well that it is very possible that you have taken a peek at these words because you find the topic of comparative religious beliefs to be fascinating in and of itself and you want to know as much as you can about the many varieties of religious belief and experience.

You may find it useful to know a little bit about me and my interest in writing this book. I am sixty years old and am a Protestant clergyman. I am the pastor of a congregation which belongs to the United Church of Christ. For the first forty five years of my life I was a Roman Catholic. During that time, I served as a Catholic high school religion teacher and a Director of Religious Education and Youth Ministry in some local Catholic parishes. I was also ordained in the Catholic Church as a Permanent Deacon (which is considered clergy) and officiated at over two hundred

1

baptisms while a Catholic, as well as a large number of marriages and funerals, as well as many other Roman Catholic rituals such as Stations of the Cross and Benediction of the Blessed Sacrament.

As a matter of fact, of the five members of my immediate family (my wife of thirty three years, my two sons and my daughter), I happen to be the only one who is not a Catholic. I also am very pleased to say that I don't consider myself an angry ex-Catholic. As one who freely and gladly identifies myself as a Protestant Christian, I am also happy to say that I am deeply grateful for my Catholic upbringing and education. As a product of Roman Catholic elementary school, preparatory school, college and some graduate school, I am forever thankful for both what I learned and how I learned it.

In my book *Crossing the Street* (Energion Publications, 2012), I explain in detail both why I left the Catholic Church and why I embraced the Protestant tradition within Christianity. I also emphasize that making this kind of decision is an intensely personal matter and I would note that I am not in the business of trying to persuade Catholics to become Protestants. Instead my interest in this topic is born of my belief, honed through my life experience, that Catholics and Protestants have so much to learn from each other and that one's own personal growth as a Christian can be deeply enriched by knowing more about the varied individual churches within the broader Christian tradition. My life as a Roman Catholic has enriched my current Protestant expression of faith. It is my hope that exposure to varieties of religious practice can deepen your own practice of faith as well.

WHAT DOES A PROTESTANT NEED TO KNOW ABOUT CATHOLICS?

In other words, what are we going to cover in this book? In order to both organize it and to do my best to make this little resource helpful, I would like to lay out some basic topics that I believe we need to explore in order to provide an adequate answer to this question:

1. What's the major difference between Protestants and Catholics?
2. What are some of the other important differences and points of emphasis within these two largest Christian groupings?
3. Do we have more in common than that which is different?

Yet before we even delve into these three extremely important areas of inquiry, we have to face a basic fact. **Neither** Protestantism nor Catholicism can be categorized easily or simply. In other words, there exists a **variety** of ways in which people are either Protestant or Roman Catholic.

Now, for Protestants, that statement might be rather obvious. We all know that under the Protestant umbrella we will find Baptists, Congregationalists, Episcopalians, Methodists, Presbyterians, and Lutherans, just to name a few. In the minds of most, to be Catholic is to simply be, well, Catholic. In reality, there is incredible variety within the different traditions of Catholicism. Where one is raised a Catholic is important and, in many cases, the ethnicity of the local parish might influence how one worships, what one emphasizes and to a great degree how one thinks about religious issues.

Students exposed to Catholic education are influenced by the approach of those who run that particular school. I offer myself as an example. The Catholic elementary school I attended was run by a group of nuns with its international headquarters in France and most of its members raised French Canadian in the United States. My prep school was staffed by Marian Fathers, a rather conservative group whose roots were in Lithuania. My college and early graduate school education occurred in institutions run by the Jesuits, whose approach to higher education is both well known and unique within the Catholic community. My collegiate experience included a deep immersion in what one could legitimately call a 'progressive' approach to the Catholic faith.

3

Likewise, in spite of the fact that Catholic positions on such matters as divorce, remarriage, homosexuality, contraception and abortion are usually seen as more traditional and conservative than what is normative in society, what people often do not realize is that there is a wide diversity of opinion within Catholicism on these issues, as well as such others as the ordination of women and married men to the priesthood.

Therefore, just as the differences in Protestantism are marked both by denomination and in approach to the Bible (as we have seen in some of the controversies about Bible interpretation, especially on social issues), a pluralism of approaches exists within the Catholic community. In *Crossing the Street,* I explore this in detail, citing the clear lines of distinction between John XXIII and John Paul II Catholics. By this categorization, I distinguish between Catholics who interpret the reforms of the Second Vatican Council differently. Where Pope Francis I fits into this is open to further development and exploration.

Now, having offered this caveat regarding the variety within these different church communities, it is now most appropriate to try our best to pin down the differences between Protestant and Catholic.

WHAT'S THE MAJOR DIFFERENCE?

Before one explores what one might call the MAJOR difference, I think it is necessary to recognize that there are a number of differences between these two church traditions. While some are born out of different points of emphasis, as in the case in different worship styles, for example, in Protestant churches, some might also very much point the way to answering the central question of what the major difference might be. It would be worthwhile to take a look at some behaviors, practices, customs and tendencies associated with being either Protestant or Catholic. What might people put on this list were they asked the question? Let's give this what is more than likely an incomplete answer, yet an answer containing worthwhile information nonetheless!! It seems to me that those responding would provide at least the following phrases concerning the identifiable Catholic tendencies:

The Virgin Mary, saints, Mass in Latin, altar boys, CCD, Catholic schools, Notre Dame football, daily Mass, Rosary, Novenas, Forty Hours, Stations of the Cross, Benediction of the Blessed Sacrament, tabernacles, votive candles, Last Rites, seven sacraments, spiritual bouquets, statues, Mary crowning, the Mary side of the sanctuary, Confession, First Communion, Marian apparitions (i.e. reported appearances such as Lourdes, Fatima, Guadalupe, Medjugorje). no marriage for priests, nuns, monks, no abortion, divorce or birth control, annulments, Bingo, the Pope, the Vatican, leaving Mass after Communion, genuflecting, receiving Jesus in Communion, scapular medals, the Sign of the Cross, holy water, Easter Duty, a lot of rules to follow.... This is probably just the start!!!

And, conversely, what might be some phrases, again incomplete as they might be, that could be associated with Protestants?:

Emphasis on the Bible, hymn singing, usually longer services than Catholics, all the verses of the hymns, many of their churches look pretty plain and simple compared to Catholic ones, all kinds of different churches and denominations, no central authority, no Pope, not much talk about Mary or 'the saints,' more leniency on divorce, remarriage, birth control and abortion, more kids go to public schools, a lot of churches on the local greens or the establishment church in the local neighborhood, Fellowship Hours, Pot Luck Luncheons, church suppers, with favorite dishes dependent on regions or denomination, Sunday School, Rally Sunday, Homecoming Sunday, more voluntary church attendance than Catholics, personal right to interpret the Bible, the religious tradition most closely connected with early America, the force behind educational institutions such as Yale and Harvard, congregations owning church property and deciding on their own ministers, not as much emphasis as Catholics on the power of the hierarchy, not as many rules as Catholics, Billy Graham, TV preachers, a more low key

Lent (with no meat restrictions!), a lot of emphasis on good preaching, tent meetings and revivals.

At first glance, this list may seem to make a case for a chasm so deep and wide that it really cannot be bridged and that we are really dealing with two separate religious cultures. My conviction, on the other hand, is that there is considerable misunderstanding among those of us who would make these identifications. These misunderstandings contribute to a great amount of inaccuracy were one to utilize these listings in order to answer the central question in this inquiry.

First of all, these lists do not identify where each practice or tendency rests in the priorities of that particular church. Nor do they take into account the historical contexts out of which some of the items listed evolved or the discussions about these topics that have emerged both within Protestant and Catholic churches and also between them. As an example, one could legitimately ask if any of these practices, in and of themselves, are really obstacles to either dialogue with or even unity with the other tradition. Maybe even more importantly, one could explore the range of interpretations regarding these practices that might exist within the traditions themselves. Certainly, as a Catholic clergyperson, I was aware that the devotion of Benediction of the Blessed Sacrament was less important to some Catholics than to others and that there are those who call themselves Catholic for whom Benediction would rate low on the hierarchical ladder of cherished Catholic beliefs. Recent stories in the religious press have reinforced this perspective.

In the same vein, contemporary Protestantism has a diversity of views on social and sexual issues. While Catholicism has been identified with the movement against abortion, there are large pockets of such sentiment within Protestant churches today.

All of this being said, it would be dishonest to claim that there are no differences and to yield to a bland religious indifferentism. They **do** matter. In my own life, I made the decision to move away from Roman Catholicism and to become a Protestant because I experienced some differences. And, even as I contend, as I do, that my decision is intended not as a universal one, but rather as my own, it can only make sense to **me** if I am able to identify the reality that there are differences and that whatever affirmations I might make can only be made with a personal recognition of what those differences are. The acknowledgment of difference then should **never** be an obstacle to either dialogue or unity. In fact, I am convinced that instead it can function as a major contributor to what our common church needs!

THE ROMAN CATHOLIC DIFFERENCE:
THE QUESTION OF AUTHORITY

When all is said and done, there **is** a distinguishing difference between Roman Catholic Christianity and other Christian traditions, including both the Orthodox churches and all Protestants. This major difference is connected to a number of the other differences one might see when comparing different churches. *Simply put, it is the Catholic Church alone which acknowledges the specific authority of the Pope.*

In other words, Roman Catholics believe that the Bishop of Rome has a unique place among all of the other bishops and is ultimately the source of earthly authority for the church. This is based, according to Catholic understanding, on the declaration to Peter that 'You are rock and upon this rock will I build my church' (Matthew 16:18). In Catholicism, the Pope is seen as the successor to Peter and exercises Petrine authority, i.e. the primary leadership function in the church. This authority extends to church teachings, specific church laws and the specifics of church governance. It also explains the 'Roman' in Roman Catholic, with the Petrine ministry centered in the Bishop of Rome. *No major declaration of faith in the name of the Catholic Church can be released without the approval of the Pope.* Church laws (specifically the comprehensive Code of

Canon Law) require Papal approval to be put into effect. All other bishops in the church are appointed by the Pope as well as all of the Cardinals who will eventually be the electors for any future Popes.

In stating this understanding of the place of the Bishop of Rome in Catholic life, it is likewise important to make the following clear:

1. Other churches have bishops (e.g. Anglicans, Lutherans, Methodists). The Bishop of Rome holds a unique place within Catholicism in comparison with these other bishops.
2. Not all Catholics are in agreement on issues regarding **how** the Pope should be selected or what the parameters of his authority should be. The question of Papal infallibility, i.e. that the Pope speaks infallibly for the whole church when he speaks on matters of faith and morals is one that has been intensely debated since its designation as church teaching by the First Vatican Council in 1870.
3. The Papacy as it is presently constructed does not necessarily represent the Papacy within the first several centuries of Christianity. In the same way, certain Popes emphasize various aspects of the Petrine (Papal) function. This was most apparent in the differences between John XXIII and John Paul II and is currently becoming noticeable during the brief tenure thus far of Pope Francis I.

Having said all of this, it **is** fair to say that to be Roman Catholic, whether one deems oneself a Catholic traditionalist or progressive, involves affirming the importance of the Pope as integral to the life of the church. Reform minded Catholics might yearn for changes in certain policies or insist that the Pope act and deliberate in collegial conjunction with other bishops, yet would nonetheless affirm the ministry of the Bishop of Rome as *essential* to the Catholic faith. *Protestant Christianity does not share in this affirmation.*

Protestant Christians, on the other hand, might admire the work of a particular Pope or might see the value and importance of having an internationally recognized spokesperson for Christianity. Some might even go so far as to yearn for a day when a leader could be accepted by both Catholics and Protestants alike. Yet, in spite of any of that, Protestant Christians would *not* see the role of the Pope as essential to the structuring and ordering of the visible church of Jesus Christ on earth.

From a Catholic perspective, the authority of the Pope rests upon what is written in the Bible. From a Protestant approach, the Catholic position has added layers of interpretation to the words that Jesus spoke to Peter. Protestants would argue that it is one thing to call Peter a rock upon which the church would be founded and yet another to claim that Peter's successors would have ultimate control over what the universal church would teach in Jesus' name, the laws that would govern it, and the individuals who would be appointed to positions of authority within it.

DIFFERENCE AND DIFFERENCES

It is important to note that while we contend that the authority of the Pope is a distinguishing characteristic within the Catholic Church and the major difference between Catholics and Protestants, it is also necessary to recognize that there **are** differences in other areas as well. These areas might include specific ways of worshiping or unique traditions that have been passed down through the generations. One could legitimately contend that there **are** Catholic tendencies and a Catholic way of seeing things which has had an impact upon those who have been raised in the Catholic tradition. Over the next several pages, I will seek to make this statement clearer.

We must also repeat what was stated earlier. An individual's understanding of her/his Catholicism has been shaped by the specific context in which s/he has experienced Catholicism. It is equally fair to say that an individual Protestant could say that about her/his Lutheranism or Presbyterian faith, for example, as well. Differences between and among members of churches might exist even in churches where people might freely share a common core of faith or doctrine. I can state from personal experience as a Catholic how many lively discussions I participated in with my fellow Catholics. These conversations dealt with a great variety of controversial issues about which not all Catholics agreed!

Nonetheless, one cannot escape the fact that an understanding of the Petrine ministry as essential to the church represents the distinguishing distinctive characteristic of Catholicism, one that has built-in implications for some of the other differences as well.

Over these next few pages, we are going to examine some other significant Catholic tendencies and practices, how they are related to core Catholic questions and what their real impact is on the life of individual Catholics as well as the Catholic Church. It is my hope that in doing so, the reader who is not a Catholic will gain a deeper insight into the complexities and the nuances of Catholic faith.

AUTHORITY IN EVERYDAY CATHOLIC LIFE

As a Protestant clergyman in a local church in which I was selected for my job by the congregation, I am part of a structure in which a good amount of decision making authority belongs to the members of the local congregation itself. If my church is displeased with how I preach or the use of my time, they could make the decision to fire me and then call another pastor.

In practical terms, if you are a Catholic and you are not thrilled with the work of your pastor and if his competence is so low or his behavior so appalling that it would be best for him to leave your church, you cannot be directly involved in the decision because in the Roman Catholic system of governance, that is the job of the local bishop and those church officials who have been assigned by him to deal with personnel matters.

Fortunately, since the years of the Second Vatican Council, many Catholic dioceses have sought to engage members of local churches in the process of offering input. Unfortunately, many have not. In either case, any ultimate decision cannot and will not be made by the 'laypersons' who belong to the local church. Their church property itself will not be owned by them either. Local church buildings and cemeteries in the church's name will very likely be owned by the local diocese, under the control of the local bishop.

The style of governance within the Catholic Church is hierarchical, with the Pope at the center of the hierarchy. Popes appoint bishops. Bishops ordain priests and deacons and assign them to local parishes. Priests exercise hierarchical authority over deacons in their settings, though deacons serve at the discretion of the bishop. The understanding of deacon as an ordained position is in keeping with the hierarchical understanding within Catholic faith and practice. Over the course of time, enormous power has been granted to those holding the position of priest, especially those who are local church pastors.

As a Protestant pastor who works in a denomination where there are many former Catholics, I have seen first hand and up close the tendency of ex-Catholics to expect from me what they would get from a Catholic pastor. In many Catholic settings, the member of the parish who has a request 'seeks permission' from the priest for this to be allowed. The pastor exerts much direct control over the everyday workings of the local Catholic church. In my context and within much of Protestantism, the pastor's own personal authority does not extend into certain areas of church decision making, which might be in the hands of church trustees or Council members, depending upon the situation. I am expected to weigh

11

in on matters and have some influence, **but** I do not possess the authority to **decide**.

This understanding of authority extends into the area of moral teaching as well. Most people who follow political issues in the United States are well aware of the fact that Catholic leaders have taken strong public stances on a good number of issues, including opposition to legalized abortion, certain health care policies that endorse contraception, and same sex marriage.

The belief that the Catholic Church possesses a teaching authority (*magisterium* is the technical Catholic term) which is intended to clarify moral issues for Catholics is a significant one within the Catholic framework. Those who are not Catholic have often been troubled that the Catholic Church has a high comfort level with imposing its own beliefs upon those who may hold different ones in a pluralistic society, abortion being a case in point. Many Catholics see church leaders speaking out on issues and expecting certain responses from Catholic laity as a legitimate exercise of their teaching authority.

The Catholic Church has traditionally held that, within its teaching authority, its leaders are not only providing moral guidance to the broader society, but also operating within what is obliged of them, i.e. that they interpret the Scripture and promulgate the natural law for those who call themselves Roman Catholic.

An honest look at this matter requires that we recognize what is most likely the clearest example of how this principle has clashed with the experience of everyday Catholics. In 1968, after a lengthy period of discussion and study, the Pope at that time, Paul VI, declared that the use of contraception (birth control) is immoral. He did so in his encyclical *Humanae Vitae*. This declaration came at a time when birth control use was becoming increasingly common in many societies and amidst a hope and expectation among Catholics that the church's position might change.

Because the Pope, and thus the church, held to the traditional belief, some have asserted that a situation developed wherein the **lived experience** of ordinary, faithful Catholics came head to head with the **teaching authority** of the church in a way that had profound impact upon their lives and their marriages. Interestingly enough, in the period leading up to this encyclical, and even subsequently, it was not unusual for Catholic women to seek out the counsel of understanding Catholic priests for the purpose of 'getting permission' to use birth control. This notion of obtaining permission from a clergyperson is not ordinarily part of the Protestant experience and speaks to the relationship with church authority that has traditionally been part of the Catholic experience.

This chasm between official church teaching and the belief of ordinary Catholics has widened in the years since the birth control encyclical. All available data shows that Catholic couples practice birth control as much as non Catholics and that they have comparable abortion rates as well. The attitudes of most Catholics today clash with official teachings on homosexuality, divorce and remarriage, and several other issues as well.

There is a living tension within the Catholic Church between those who define Catholic in terms of strict adherence to specific teaching and others who hold to the position that dissenting positions taken in good conscience are part of the Catholic tradition as well. These differences are evident in the diversity of opinions and approaches that have existed among Catholic priests, pastoral ministers and theologians over the years. During the pontificates of John Paul II and Benedict XVI in recent years, major initiatives were taken to weed out much of this diversity. Theologians were stripped of their rights to teach Catholic theology, books were banned, and those who had shown any evidence of dissent were not appointed as bishops. Under John Paul II, the church issued a comprehensive new catechism, an attempt to clarify and codify the fundamental teachings of the faith and to draw a line with respect to dissenters.

So, at this point in time, if you are a Protestant looking in from the outside at the Catholic Church, you need to be aware that from the time of the Second Vatican Council (1962-1965) and through the years that have ensued since the birth control encyclical in 1968, the Catholic Church has experienced the following:

1. Strong attempts from the Pope and bishops to adopt uniformity in teaching and practice.
2. Continued resistance from other professionals within the church and from 'people in the pews' who have dissented quietly, following an approach to Catholicism that respects individual conscience, even against the official church declarations.
3. A decline in church attendance and participation among great numbers of those who were raised within the Catholic Church, often including movement into other Christian denominations. This often occurs around issues of divorce and remarriage and the raising of children, though it is most certainly not limited to those matters.

As we look carefully now at other Catholic tendencies and points of emphasis, you will see how this underlying issue of authority has a significant place in many other areas of Catholic life.

IMPORTANT CATHOLIC TENDENCIES AND POINTS OF EMPHASIS

One who is seeking to learn more about Catholicism needs to be aware of the fact that there are several aspects of Catholicism of which one must be cognizant in order to get a full and clear picture of this approach to Christian faith. These tendencies and points of emphasis are not as integral to distinguishing Catholicism from Protestantism as the matter of papal authority. Nevertheless, they are strong indicators of the lived experience of being Catholic and important for non-Catholics as they seek to understand not only 'the Catholic tradition,' but also those who have been and are a part of it. In this section, I have identified what I see as several key 'must knows' for those who seek to know more. While I won't say they are exhaustive, it is my hope that they will point you in the right directions:

1. THE MASS

The distinguishing public worship event within Catholicism is popularly known as 'The Mass.' It is also called the celebration of the Eucharist and the central action in it leads to the reception of Communion. While many Protestant churches offer Communion once a month, in the Catholic Church the ideal worship service is the Mass, plain and simple. For a very long time, the expectation among Catholics has been that daily Mass would be available in local parishes. For many, attending daily Mass is part of their ordinary Lenten practice, though it is not required by Catholic law.

With the decline in priests, grave concerns have been expressed that people are not able to attend Mass and receive Communion. The Catholic Church has developed processes whereby parishioners may receive Communion in services held in the absence of a priest, with Communion elements that have been consecrated by a priest at another Mass. Even among liberal Catholics, this importance of the Mass is cited as evidence for why married priests should be available to celebrate the Eucharist. It is not unusual for those Catholics who attend Protestant worship to have a sense of incompleteness if Communion is not celebrated as part of the service.

There are a number of reasons why the centrality of the Mass developed within the Catholic tradition. Much of it comes from the official church teaching that in the Mass, one receives in Communion 'the body and blood of Christ.' Catholics traditionally believe that this is effected through the actions of an ordained priest, one ordained by a bishop in apostolic succession, dating back to Peter, whom Jesus selected. Built into this is the sense that, in his ministry at the altar and in the church, the priest serves as an *alter Christus,* i.e. another Christ.

Even among those Protestants raised in churches where Communion was celebrated weekly, much of this Catholic understanding is seen as somewhat different from their own. Within those traditions which emphasize that Jesus is, in some way, truly present in Communion, the view of the ordained minister's role is different from the Catholic position.

Many Protestants I have known have expressed to me a certain discomfort in receiving Communion in a Catholic Church. Much of this feeling has centered on a concern that they really are not welcomed. This is reinforced by some priests who make it quite clear that only Catholics are invited to the Communion table. The printed worship materials used in many Catholic parishes explicitly state this stipulation.

The official legal position of the Catholic Church does not necessarily reflect the mindset of a large number of practicing Catholics. Many Catholics are most comfortable receiving Communion at Protestant services on occasion as well. Many Catholics, however, **do** articulate the concern that since Communion is supposed to represent unity of faith and visible unity does not exist between Protestants and Catholics, sharing Communion in that case is not really the sign which it claims to be.

On the other hand, many Catholics and Protestants alike sense a strong **spiritual** unity with each other. It is this unity that transcends any differences between and among the churches on either the outward unity of the church or the specific nature of what happens to the elements during the service of Communion. Contrary to what many people think, Protestant and Catholic theologians in dialogue have reached significant agreements regarding Communion. These agreements render some of the old divisions on some of the issues surrounding Communion as open to question.

As I note above, Catholicism has for centuries embraced the tradition of 'daily Mass,' one which is still maintained in many places. As a Catholic college student in the 1970's, daily Mass was part of my routine. An underlying traditional concept within Catholicism is that Mass has an effect on others, including those who have died and are in purgatory. Thus, it is typical when you look at a Catholic bulletin to see a Mass schedule with several listings 'for the repose of the soul' of one who has died. While not being the primary purpose for celebrating Mass, there **is** a linkage between this celebration and Catholic beliefs about praying for the dead, which are different from Protestant understanding.

In the past several decades there has been considerable growth both in the Protestant understanding and appreciation of the Communion service and in Catholicism's self reflection upon the Eucharist. Having said this, the celebration of Mass is a ritual that has a deep emotional connection for those who are part of the Catholic experience. It is for them the *normative* mode of public worship.

2.   OTHER RITUALS AND RITUAL ACTIONS

Among the many examples of particular words and phrases that people think of when thinking about Catholicism, including the ones I indicated earlier in this book, a large number center on particular rituals or ritual actions--certain prayers, ways of praying (e.g. Stations of the Cross, the Rosary) and particular individual and family celebrations that are part of Catholic life, a noteworthy example being that of First Communion.

Of course, every religious tradition is marked by its own unique set of rituals. One could do an overview of major world religions and find considerable evidence for this claim. Thus it is very important to get some kind of handle on the place of ritual in Catholic life.

It is likewise necessary to recognize that not all rituals have the same adherence and impact among all Catholics. Particular devotions and prayers associated with different feast days or saints may be more popular in some Catholic contexts than in others.

An example would be devotions centered on saints recognized by particular ethnic communities e.g. St. Patrick for the Irish, St. Anthony for Italians. In addition, there are good numbers of Catholics whose prayer life involves very little to no time at all spent in such devotional practices.

Yet, even recognizing this, we need to say that the very existence of devotions centered around certain saints might be something new for many Protestants to discover and comprehend. In many Catholic churches, statues of these saints are present and in most Catholic parishes, you will find a statue of Mary in a relatively prominent place.

Among traditional Catholics, many of these devotions consist of certain prayers and routines. The Protestant Christian might have difficulty understanding the value and importance attached to aspects of the religion that are not Christ centered. What is important to recognize is that within Catholicism, there is a continuum of attitude and practice toward these devotions, including perhaps the most noteworthy, the Rosary. Not all Catholics are devotion centered; many are. As with many aspects of Catholic practice, there is a surprising variety and pluralism when it comes to the worldwide church.

The First Communion ritual, a surprisingly recent development in Roman Catholicism, is one most Protestants will find to be unlike any other they have experienced. In most American Catholic homes, it is one of the most important family occasions in the course of a child's lifetime. Depending on the local parish, it may be a simple ceremony or an elaborate multifaceted ritual. It **does** tend to be one of those ceremonial experiences *missed* by former Catholics who switch over to Protestant churches.

More progressive Catholics will emphasize that none of these traditions is really required in order to be Catholic. More traditional Catholics will stress that young people should not be denied exposure to them. Protestants exploring the Catholic Church will usually find themselves with a lot of questions. What is important to understand is that more important than some of these particular actions are those seven actions that Catholics view as SACRA-MENTS—Baptism, Confirmation, Eucharist, Reconciliation, Matrimony, Holy Orders, and the Sacrament of the Sick.

The essence of each of these actions that one will find in Catholic sacraments is found within the wide range of ritual actions within Protestant churches. There **is** a quarrel over terminology between traditional Catholics and Protestants, i.e. regarding what constitutes a **sacrament**. Likewise, one who is not a Catholic may be surprised when he/she learns of certain **laws** attached to the celebration of sacraments. Examples of this include the fasting regulation prior to reception of Communion as well as the obligation that one must be in a 'state of grace' prior to receiving that sacrament. 'State of grace' refers to the absence of any unconfessed 'mortal sin,' i.e. a sin that is considered gravely serious in nature. Of course there is disagreement among Catholics regarding what constitutes such a grievous matter. Examples of disagreement are often in the area of sexual behavior, e,g. is practicing birth control mortally sinful?

There is no quarrel, however, that in both traditions, what is celebrated in these actions: birth, commitment to Christ, commitment to another person, the healing power of God, etc. is most assuredly that which we share in common. Though ordinarily Protestants claim to celebrate two sacraments (or what some Protestants call ordinances), there is no doubt that the depth of these actions and their importance to the life of faith is shared by Catholics and Protestants alike.

3. THE IMPORTANT PLACE OF THE PRIEST IN CATHOLIC LIFE

As we have mentioned above, the role of the priest in the Catholic community is one that has been traditionally held in high regard. The power possessed by 'Father' and the respect and reverence accorded to the man holding that title has been enormous. As most of us know, over the last decade the Catholic Church has been rocked with many revelations related to sexual abuse among its priests. The very fact that priests and human sexuality have been linked together has been a difficult reality for many Catholics to face. In spite of all of the terrible crimes that have been committed by some of their priests, however, Catholics place great value upon the role of the priest. As I noted previously, even many who sought to go against the official church teaching regarding contraception were able to justify this if their priest gave his approval!

Some of this thinking about the status of priests is linked to theological reasons as found in the church's notion of authority which we have described. Some is a result of a lack of emphasis of the notion of 'priesthood of all believers' that is part of Protestant tradition. Currently much of this has been buttressed by the disillusionment of many lay persons, including a large number of women. Where in the years after Vatican II, there was strong impetus for change and for the proliferation of lay ministry positions in churches and diocese, much of this has waned and the importance of having good priests assigned to parishes has taken on even more importance in many cases.

4. THE CATHOLIC SENSE OF 'OUTSIDER'
Many young Catholics today are descendants of immigrant Catholics who came to this country from Europe. When they came, they sought to integrate themselves into an American culture which had been dominated by Protestantism. In many cases, this was not an easy assimilation. Catholic immigrants and their descendants had to deal with both blatant and subtle anti Catholicism. It is within this context that one can understand the importance of the election of John F. Kennedy as President in 1960 in the lives and self perception of American Catholics.

While this sense of outsider is less powerful and pervasive among these younger descendants, there remains in many Catholic families a strong linkage of ethnic identification with the Catholic Church, even when real life religious practice might not abide with

Catholic teaching. While strong in many ethnic groups, it appears to take on a unique significance in the Irish Catholic mindset, as Irish Catholicism has produced so many political and religious leaders as well as a large number of distinguished Catholic educational institutions, in and of themselves countercultural symbols as they were built to assert the legitimate place of Catholics in the world of academia. Notable examples include the University of Notre Dame whose football program helped propel the growth and prominence of the University on the national scene. It would also include the strong network of Jesuit institutions such as Boston College, Holy Cross and Georgetown, among several others.

The Catholic tradition has thus been most sympathetic historically to the plight of immigrants and the rights of workers. This Catholic tendency toward social justice and advocacy for the marginalized remains, even though a good number of young and middle aged Catholics tend not to perceive themselves as outsiders within the broader culture. For many older Catholics, this notion that they had to struggle to find their way against an establishment that was Protestant dominated still lingers and presents itself as an impediment to full ecumenicity.

5. THE IMPORTANCE OF 'THE CHURCH' TO CATHOLICS

For better or worse, when Catholics think of 'the church' they think of the Catholic one. Conservative Catholics may approach this on theological grounds, arguing that in Jesus' words to Peter, He founded the one true church. Other Catholics might be more moved by their church's uniqueness among other churches and the international visibility of Rome and the Pope. For some, the church's importance is caused by the enormous power it has wielded in the personal decision making places of their lives, with its laws and regulations governing a wide variety of human behavior.

In order to understand the unique Catholic gut level sense of church, we need to look at a reality within American Protestantism. It is not at all unusual among American Protestants to belong to different Protestant denominations over the course of a lifetime, to be, as example, Presbyterian in one place and Congregational in another, all without having a major internal change or feeling he or she has 'left the church.' This church switching takes place for many reasons. For example, some denominations have very little presence in some parts of the country. The Disciples of Christ, for example, which has many congregations in several locations, has very few in New England. If a member from that church moved to a particular location, he or she might not find a church of his or her native denomination. In certain local contexts, a particular church might offer better programs in areas important to an individual. This would motivate shifting church and denominational allegiance.

Some would argue that Catholicism has a strong set of creedal beliefs that are taught clearly to young Catholics as they grow up with delineated positions about the unique importance of the Catholic Church. They would say that this emphasis is less operative in Protestant denominations, despite the fact that one **will** meet many whose theology and understanding of church is clearly reflective of a strong denominational teaching influence. As examples, it is not unusual to find lifelong Lutherans or Episcopalians or Presbyterians. Nonetheless, the overall denominational grip among adherents of Protestant churches pales in comparison to that of their Catholic counterparts. Protestantism possesses a great number of churches that label themselves interdenominational, independent or nondenominational as well. These churches draw not only Protestants from different backgrounds but also those raised Catholic.

Protestantism has likewise been marked by the presence of a large number of 'federated' churches. In these churches, congregations of different denominations actually merge together into one local church community. There are many different federated configurations. One relatively local church with which I am familiar is a federation of United Church of Christ members with Congregationalist roots, Unitarian Universalists and United Methodists. Were one to go inside of the theology of these three groups, one would find some marked differences. In terms of bodies of beliefs, for example, there are clear differences between Methodist and Unitarian Universalist theology.

None of this is intended to be critical of federated churches which, in my view, contain great potential in the church of both present and future. It is rather to highlight the unique place of the Catholic Church in the Roman Catholic view of church. As an anonymous ex Catholic cited by one of my Jesuit professors once said: *"In the Catholic mind, the Catholic Church is the only church which is 'THE church.'"*

A PERSONAL NOTE

As I have noted, many years ago, I left the Catholic Church and became a Protestant. While the overwhelming majority of people whom I know were positive and supportive of my choice, a good number of Catholics had difficulty understanding it. One might think that I am referring primarily to so called 'traditional' Catholics. I am not. This sense of 'church as Catholic Church' cuts across theological divides. It does so for a variety of different reasons, for sure, yet it does nevertheless.

Even among several ecumenically-minded Catholics whom I have known, there is the understanding that it is acceptable to be Protestant if you have been raised Protestant, but why would you actually **choose** to be a Protestant if you have been raised in the Catholic Church? My intent in pointing this out is not to be critical, though I do come at these matters from a place that is different from those who would ask this question. My purpose is to point out the different ways in which the place of a particular church in one's life is understood and the uniqueness of the Catholic instinct in this regard.

23

At this point, as we draw to the end of an overview of significant Catholic tendencies, it is important that we both recognize and discuss how Protestants often perceive Catholics. In doing so, it is essential that we highlight several noteworthy misunderstandings regarding Catholicism within the broad Protestant community. As we do this, we must again be cognizant of the reality that Protestantism is not monolithic and that it contains within it many theologies, cultural contexts and personal as well as ecclesiastical histories. Having said that, it is possible to both find and comment about the ways in which Catholicism is often misunderstood.

PROTESTANT MISUNDERSTANDINGS OF CATHOLICISM

As is the case with most misunderstandings, each incomplete rendering of another's position is based on **something** that has a degree of fact attached. Such is the case with some common Protestant views about Catholicism which may not be entirely accurate. Here are several of the most common:

1. Catholicism is a religion of rules and laws. It is more important for Catholics that they obey the Pope and the teachings of the church than that they follow what is in the Bible. *This misunderstanding takes into account the **fact** that the teaching authority of the church is important in the Catholic understanding of church.* Where it is deficient is that it fails to recognize that, as many serious Catholic theologians have long contended, the place of **individual conscience** is highly valued in Catholic decision making. Of course, there is ongoing debate in the Catholic Church between those who lean toward favoring individual conscience and those who contend that well informed consciences will inevitably assent to the church's teaching. Yet, this very **tension** speaks to a pluralism within the church often not acknowledged by those outside it.

24

2. Catholicism is a guilt ridden religion. *Many Catholics and former Catholics my age and older will recall how frequent confession was part of our growing up process. We also will recognize the variety of church rules that were possible to break (missing Mass, not fasting or abstaining from meat, failing to go to confession, etc) and one cannot argue that this rule consciousness can certainly leave a residue of guilt.* Yet, even in recognizing this history and its impact on the Catholic psyche, it is also important to note the evolution in Catholic thinking regarding the place of rules in everyday Catholic life. In other words, modern Catholics are more comfortable with 'following their consciences' than were those of generations past.

   . Interestingly enough, one could legitimately argue that guilt has moved many Catholics who have strayed from church teaching into the arena of non-practicing (popularly known as 'lapsed') Catholic. Yet, even in saying that, we also see that Catholicism has instituted organized efforts to reach out to those within who feel alienated from the church because of marital status, sexual orientation or ethical choices they have made. For many years, Catholic dioceses and parishes have implemented excellent programs for divorced and remarried Catholics. There have been positive strides made to reach out to those who have had abortions, as well as to members of the gay community. Some of these outreach programs have either slowed down or taken a different turn as a result of the papacies of John Paul II and Benedict XVI.

3. Catholicism is too ritualistic. *It is clear that Roman Catholic worship has certain rubrics or directions that those leading it are expected to follow. It is also a religious tradition replete with color, statues, important symbols and rituals attached to the use of those symbols, e.g. water and oil, to name but two.* Protestants critiquing Catholics often fail to see that their own traditions have certain expectations in worship as well and that those churches that claim to be 'free' in worship are often deeply attached to

denominational or congregational traditions which, in effect, limit their freedom. Just ask any Protestant pastor who has hit a wall when trying to effect change in her/his congregation's worship service.

4. Catholics worship the saints, especially Mary. *This misconception comes from a misunderstanding of the role of the saints, including Mary, within the Catholic framework.* While intercession of the saints (i.e. saints praying for the living) is not part of Protestant tradition, what is often misunderstood is that, even in this theology, the saints pray to God. The saints are not God. There is a difference and that should be recognized even if the theological approaches are different.

5. Catholics don't pay a lot of attention to the Bible. *Protestantism was founded on the notion of 'returning to the Bible'. The proud history of Protestant faith has emphasized strong Biblical preaching.* In addition, until the vigorous church renewal of Vatican II, Catholicism tended to lag behind Protestantism in terms of training its preachers. Yet, what is important to realize is that this has changed! Just as one example, I can point out that my homiletic training as a Catholic Permanent Deacon was superb, as have been the programs in place in Catholic seminaries which, in many cases, have been run in ecumenical conjunction with Protestant homiletic programs as well. Likewise, the fundamentalist strain in Biblical scholarship has been more clearly a Protestant phenomenon than a Catholic one. In fact, Catholic Bible scholars are well read among Protestant seminarians and pastors.

A Protestant's Look at Catholic Strengths

In my view, when Protestants look at the Catholic Church, we need to recognize that we are looking at a church community with several significant strengths. I list the following as worthy of serious consideration:

1. A history directly traceable to the time of Jesus.
2. A strong focus on the concept of unity within the church.
3. A deep seated recognition of the importance of human ritual, including the value of art and meaningful symbols.
4. A strong organized system of both education and human services.
5. A long standing tradition of 'caring for the least.'

SUGGESTIONS AND
PRACTICAL STRATEGIES

For those of us who seek to live out our Christian faith and who are deeply cognizant of the fact that what we believe has strong implications for action, it is important and necessary that we have clear, practical strategies to put into practice our lofty ideals. Throughout these pages, I have tried to demonstrate the importance of Protestants and Catholics seeking to understand one another better than we have.

In the process of a Roman Catholic learning more about Protestantism, the Catholic is of necessity required to come to terms with what Catholicism is in all of its fullness and complexity. The same holds true for the Protestant who seeks to learn about the Roman Catholic faith. While doing such is laudable and of great value, the reality is that in actual ecclesiastical life it simply does not happen enough. Practical efforts toward such learning and consequential mutual understanding simply do not exist at the local parish/congregation level in the way that they should. It is my strong conviction that this must change for the well being of the universal church!

As I have discussed at length in my book *Crossing the Street*, a good deal of my religious formation occurred as a young person in the years during and just after the Second Vatican Council. During

27

that time period, there was a great deal of excitement among Protestants and Catholics regarding learning more about the other. There was a significant proliferation in the number of local clergy groups in which both Catholic and Protestant clergy were involved and those groups were quite active in seeking ways to promote local ecumenical activity.

It has been my experience as both a Catholic and Protestant clergyman that the fervor for this kind of activity has waned. Sadly, I have sensed that many have even considered it irrelevant and not worth the time and effort. Local clergy associations, if they are active at all, tend to focus on limited events in their local communities. They may offer a town or neighborhood wide Thanksgiving, Baccalaureate, Christmas or Easter Service but, in fact, not really do much else. Please understand: The efforts to coordinate these services are praiseworthy. I have witnessed firsthand how they have provided significant experiences for those who have attended. My argument here is that, good as these efforts truly are, Protestants and Catholics need to work alike to do more.

*I wish to encourage all 'local' gatherings of churches, whether that means town, city, or neighborhood, to work **intentionally** toward the goal of understanding those local churches which come from a different tradition than one's own.* The key word in this is the word INTENTIONALLY. I encourage local churches to place this goal front and center and to examine how ecumenical alliances may be formed to make this possible, alliances not simply comprised of 'clergy associations', important as they can be, but of believers from different traditions joining together and committing to establishing structures and programs to move toward this goal.

A parallel suggestion is that these churches and their members look toward defining and expressing the ecumenical center of which we have spoken. In other words, local Christians can be assisted in identifying those points of UNIFICATION between and among the traditions. To the fullest extent possible, local Christians should be encouraged to look for areas of unity even if they differ on particular theological points or

28

approaches to ritual. Shared statements of agreed upon beliefs constitute a positive start in this regard. These covenants can become part of the fabric of local inter-congregational life across denominational lines.

It is important to note that I do NOT advocate watering down one's core beliefs or yielding on one's legitimate and conscientious convictions. Instead, I encourage all involved to do everything humanly possible to keep avenues of dialogue open. I AM concerned that those on the Religious Right, Catholic and Protestant alike, are highly susceptible for labeling those of a more progressive or even centrist approach as possessing something 'less than the true faith.' Conversely, it is extremely difficult for someone of a more progressive bent to be at ease with a fundamentalist position. *It strikes me that in those situations, those within both approaches need to focus upon what unites them as Christians while maintaining a spirit of civility and shared respect.*

It seems clear to me that among the majority of Catholics and Protestants, there exists a solid common core of belief upon which individuals and church communities can definitely build. This includes and is not limited to the following beliefs that Protestants and Catholics share in common:

1. Belief in the existence of God.
2. Belief in Jesus Christ as revelation of God.
3. Affirmation of God as Creator, Redeemer and Sanctifier. In traditional terms, this is 'Father, Son, and Holy Spirit'.
4. Commitment to following the teachings of Jesus with respect to how we view and treat others.
5. Importance of the community of the church and the spiritual unity of those who call themselves Christians.

It is important that opportunities be provided both to clear away misunderstandings and to help individuals come to a recognition of the gifts each tradition brings the other. It is my strong contention that this is all doable through concrete and practical action based on solid principle.

It is in this spirit that I wish to offer these suggestions. Most of them are directed at what local congregations, Protestant and Catholic, can be doing **together** beginning **right now**. Some have implications, of course, for interaction and cooperation along wider denominational and church levels.

These suggestions are based on intentional changes within programs that are, for the most part, preexisting in local parishes and congregations. These all fall within the general areas of either a church's educational ministry.

My suggestion is that Catholic and Protestant congregations make DELIBERATE, ECUMENICAL efforts which might include some or most of the following:

a. In the area of what is commonly known as 'CCD' or 'Sunday School' or 'Church School,' children should be exposed to both themes of Christian unity and to the reality that there are other Christians within the broader family of Christians. In addition to specific references to Bible passages promoting such unity e.g. John 17, teachers should look for ways to cite examples and to elicit from students what they know about the churches of friends who might go to other places or buildings to do what they are doing: to learn about Jesus and to worship God. As appropriate, children might be encouraged to bring their friends with them to visit them in class and to worship at their church. Teachers should be attentive to being very positive and affirmative regarding the other churches which call themselves 'Christian.' I would also suggest that religious educators help students identify the variety of Christian churches within their own locality. This can be done through simple assignments, including walking or driving through neighborhoods and interviewing those from different churches.

On a more institutional level, it would be advisable for directors of Catholic or Protestant Christian education programs to find formal ways to meet with one another, to pray together and to construct age appropriate programming that would focus on and advance the cause of Christian unity. A natural program for young children would be an ecumenical Vacation Bible School. The very selection of materials would be a worthwhile venture in understanding worship practices in other churches. I recall serving as director of a Catholic VBS in which we utilized material from a Lutheran publishing house. The materials offered an illustration of a woman pastor offering Communion to young people at worship. For a Roman Catholic child, this is generally outside of the range of her/his church experience. First of all, this person is referred to as 'pastor,' not priest. Secondly, she is a she! Addressing these issues was valuable even within the context of a specifically Catholic catechetical environment. It would be all the more so in an ecumenical context.

This affirmation can be extended to healthy discussions of the Christian ecumenism within their own homes. It is quite possible that childrens' parents are married to or in serious relationship with those of another Christian tradition or may be an interfaith couple. Perhaps some of you reading this right now are in that situation! Recognizing this and using it as a 'teachable moment' in the context of Christian as well as basic human unity would be quite worthwhile.

Even on the younger level, opportunities can be provided for children to worship in other churches and for pastors or other leaders in other local Christian churches to come by and speak to the children. *The creative, intentional work of an ecumenical local leadership can lead to creative and valuable local actions that benefit the spiritual growth of children and strengthen the ecumenical center.*

b. The area of youth ministry provides opportunities appropriate to the age and developmental growth of these young people within the congregation. Most youth ministry programs in churches which baptize infants include Confirmation programs. Confirmation programs, in my view, should include what they traditionally do i.e .provide a serious examination of one's own church/denominational tradition. This ought to be conducted non-apologetically i.e. without attempt to convince youth that this way is the only way! Likewise, the Confirmation period should also provide opportunity for candidates to explore the theology and practice of other Christian traditions. This can be accomplished by developing joint programs with local churches, perhaps even including combined retreats staffed by members of different local faith communities. This can also be accomplished in working with youth programs in those churches which practice the baptism of older children or 'believers.'

Young people of any religious tradition deserve the opportunity to engage in dialogue with others who share their Christian conviction yet who come from a different heritage. As I have mentioned, I have spent many years involved in the area of youth ministry and my experience has been that Christian churches are far too segregated in this regard. For the most part, church youth groups meet with themselves in the comfort of their local churches. Now, there is nothing wrong with this, per se, in terms of establishing a foundation, but it remains limited if one seeks to be intentional about Christian ecumenism.

Many denominations seek to provide opportunities for their youth from different churches within that denomination to get together. This has been the basis of the long standing Catholic Youth Organization (CYO), the Sodality and denominational efforts by Protestant churches. When I was director of Christian education at a local UCC church, we joined other local UCC churches and did cooperative youth ministry together. There is much good in this. It is important to strengthen denominational identity and to communicate to youth the theology and values of a denomination. Camps and conference centers run by different churches serve this purpose well. This is all very, very good, but, in terms of strengthening the bonds of Christian unity, it still falls short of the ideal.

When I was involved as a youth minister in a Catholic Church in a small Connecticut city, I was fortunate to participate in what I consider to be a really exciting venture which, though imperfect, provides a structure upon which to build. During this time, several local Christian churches of different denominations would host 'Youth Evenings' that were structured in this way: High School age youth from the dozen or so churches would gather at one of the churches (the ideal is to rotate) on a Sunday evening at around 5:00. There would be a variety of recreational activities available and then food (usually pizza, an ecumenical staple!!). Following this, the young people would be broken up (deliberately so as to foster church diversity) and be part of a structured discussion which would involve faith sharing and examining Christian responses to certain important topics. After this, there would be a short, shared worship time, using varied worship forms, usually coordinated by the host church. Now I am back in that same city and am deeply engaged in similar work as a Protestant pastor.

In my view, this is a good model because it provides both a natural setting for interaction and structured exposure to ecumenical encounter. Its implementation was and has been far from perfect. More could be done to infuse some education regarding various facets of Christian theology and more can be developed to have the youth work in shared mission projects together, but this model does provide an *intentional* approach to ecumenism that helps young people get an inside look at other young peoples' Christian church experiences and the opportunity to articulate their own! I use the word intentional, well, **intentionally**, as I am advocating for people to really be *passionate* about the importance of this enterprise for the well being of the church!

I can not leave this section without telling you one of my favorite stories ....

It was a beautiful sunny afternoon in the year 2000 when I, in my relatively new role as director of Christian education at a Protestant church, stood outside that church's front door waiting to let in the crowds gathered to witness our youth ministry's production of the incredible play Godspell.

As I waited to open the door, I could not believe what I was seeing on that gorgeous afternoon. As I spoke with a large group from the local Catholic Church who were waiting to get in, I noticed that in the lower lot came a van of teenagers from the Methodist Church in town, followed soon thereafter by youthful representatives of a good variety of denominations, reflecting the ecumenical composition of the cast that performed this wonderful musical itself. When I turned to my right and saw a group of Episcopal youth walking from over the hill, I asked that someone else stay by the door as I ran to find our incredible director, my good friend Joe, to tell him about this amazing ecumenical moment.

What happened that weekend as we produced *Godspell* is something I will never forget. It happened again that next year as two of our youth wrote and then produced their original play *Believer*, again with a widespread ecumenical cast of young people who found in these plays and in subsequent ones they would perform together a place where they could safely bring their questions about faith and doubt and religious tradition, all to a place where they could experience all of this TOGETHER, in a remarkable spirit of this elusive entity we call Christian unity! It is a day I will never forget, a day that expresses what I believe: Protestants and Catholic together, seekers all, finding something REAL in the Gospel of Jesus Christ, somehow preparing for one another the very way of their Lord!

CONCLUSION

As I said at the very beginning, for some reason you decided to pick up this little book. Whatever that reason might be, I hope that the words contained within it have been helpful to you. I also hope and pray that, if you are so moved, you will advocate for real ecumenical efforts to kindle the fires of Christian unity in your own local area and in those contexts that are part of your life. As a matter of fact, I strongly encourage you to find away to formulate discussion groups within your church or between and among local churches to discuss the topics you have read about right here. On the following page, I list several books that I would suggest if you wish to explore Catholic faith in more detail. I encourage you to consider reading them and that they are of help to you in that unique religious journey and quest that forms the very heart and soul of your God graced life!

SUGGESTED READING

Abbott, Walter,ed. *The Documents of Vatican II.* New York: America Press, 1966.

Carroll, James. *Practicing Catholic.* Boston: Houghton Mifflin, 2009

Kavanaugh, James. *A Modern Priest Looks at His Outdated Church.* New York:Penguin, 1969.

Kung, Hans. *On Being a Christian.* New York: Doubleday, 1976

LaRochelle, Robert. *Crossing the Street.* Gonzalez, Florida: Energion Publications, 2012.

Libreria Editrice Vaticana. *Catechism of the Catholic Church.* Liguori, Mo: Liguori Publications, 1994.

McBrien, Richard. *Catholicism.* Minneapolis : Winston Press, 1981

O'Brien, David. *The Renewal of American Catholicism.* New York: Paulist Press, 1972.

MORE FROM ENERGION PUBLICATIONS

Personal Study

Finding My Way in Christianity	Herold Weiss	$16.99
The Jesus Paradigm	David Alan Black	$17.99
When People Speak for God	Henry Neufeld	$17.99

Christian Living

Faith in the Public Square	Robert D. Cornwall	$16.99
Grief: Finding the Candle of Light	Jody Neufeld	$8.99
Crossing the Street	Robert LaRochelle	$16.99

Bible Study

Learning and Living Scripture	Lentz/Neufeld	$12.99
From Inspiration to Understanding	Edward W. H. Vick	$24.99
Luke: A Participatory Study Guide	Geoffrey Lentz	$8.99
Philippians: A Participatory Study Guide	Bruce Epperly	$9.99
Ephesians: A Participatory Study Guide	Robert D. Cornwall	$9.99
Evidence for the Bible	Elgin Hushbeck, Jr.	

Theology

Creation in Scripture	Herold Weiss	$12.99
Creation: the Christian Doctrine	Edward W. H. Vick	$12.99
Ultimate Allegiance	Robert D. Cornwall	$9.99
History and Christian Faith	Edward W. H. Vick	$9.99
The Church Under the Cross	William Powell Tuck	$11.99
The Journey to the Undiscovered Country	William Powell Tuck	$9.99
Eschatology: A Participatory Study Guide	Edward W. H. Vick	$9.99
Philosophy for Believers	Edward W. H. Vick	$14.99
Christianity and Secularism	Elgin Hushbeck, Jr.	$16.99

Ministry

Clergy Table Talk	Kent Ira Groff	$9.99
Out of This World	Darren McClellan	$24.99

Generous Quantity Discounts Available
Dealer Inquiries Welcome
Energion Publications — P.O. Box 841
Gonzalez, FL_ 32560
Website: http://energionpubs.com
Phone: (850) 525-3916